Exploring Change:
Social and Cultural Progress

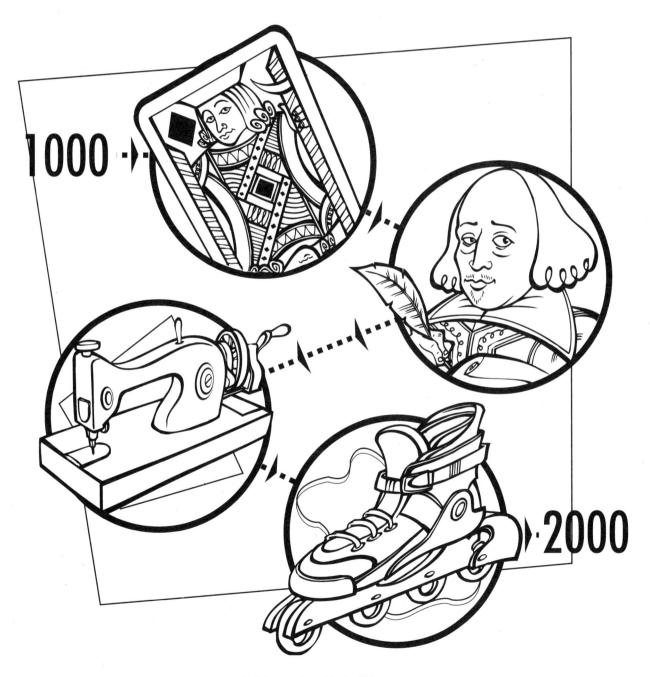

Written by Deb Nitert
Published by World Teachers Press®

Published with the permission of R.I.C. Publications Pty. Ltd.

Copyright © 2000 by Didax, Inc., Rowley, MA 01969. All rights reserved.

First published by R.I.C. Publications Pty. Ltd., Perth, Western Australia. Revised by Didax Educational Resources.

Distributed in Canada by Scholar's Choice.

Limited reproduction permission: The publisher grants permission to individual teachers who have purchased this book to reproduce the blackline masters as needed for use with their own students. Reproduction for an entire school or school district or for commercial use is prohibited.

Printed in the United States of America.

Order Number 2-5147
ISBN 1-58324-074-8

A B C D E F 03 02 01 00

395 Main Street
Rowley, MA 01969
www.worldteacherspress.com

Foreword

Exploring Change provides you with high interest mini-themes for this essential element of most Social Studies curricula. The last thousand years have brought about significant social and cultural developments and this series uses a literacy approach to explore such aspects of life as:

- toys
- transportation
- clothing
- disasters
- technology
- inventions
- food
- medicine
- communications

These topics are then developed using a variety of activities, including:

- comprehension at three levels
- word study
- research and discussion
- creative activities

Exploring Change can be incorporated into the key learning areas of English or Studies of Society and Culture.

Books in this series are:
Exploring Change – Grades 3–4
Exploring Change – Grades 5–6
Exploring Change – Grades 7–8

Contents

Teachers Notes	4 – 5
Authors	6 – 9
Clothing	10 – 13
Communication	14 – 17
Cooking	18 – 21
Energy	22 – 25
Farming	26 – 29
Medicine	30 – 33
Sea Exploration	34 – 37
Toys and Games	38 – 41
Transportation	42 – 45
Answers	46 – 48

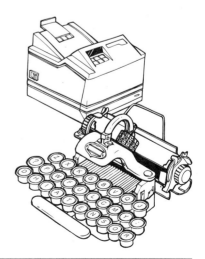

Teachers Notes

Exploring Change – Grades 5–6 contains 10 topics. Each topic has four pages covering the following areas:

- Fact sheet
- Comprehension activities
- Word study activities
- Creative activities

Topic – Authors

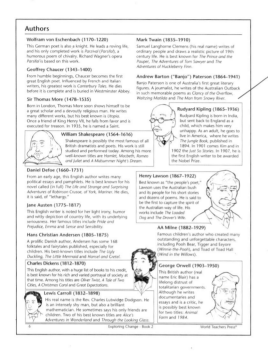

Page One of each topic is a fact sheet. It contains information and illustrations about the topic over the last millennium. The text provides students with the basis for completion of activities on the next three pages of the topic.

Introduce the topic of authors by brainstorming, in small groups, what the students know about various authors. Share knowledge and point out any deficits in information. Discuss what the students would like to know more about.

Read the text. Highlight any difficult words and discuss meaning. Encourage students to read around the word to solve any problems for themselves. Add any difficult words to personal or class dictionaries.

Read the text again and underline key facts and important information.

Discuss any new information the students have gained from the text.

Page Two contains comprehension activities at three levels. All answers can be inferred from the text.

Read each question with the class following on their own copies.

Discuss the questions, the type of questions and where students may be able to find the answers.

Re-read the text to clarify the questions. Once students have the questions in mind, reading the text will then make it easier for students to focus on specific information in the text.

Model answers on the chalkboard, demonstrating how you expect students to answer the questions. Students then work independently to answer the questions on the worksheet.

You can choose to collect and correct the work, or students can correct their own work through group discussion.

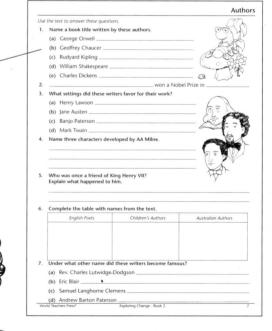

4   Exploring Change - Book 2   World Teachers Press®

Teachers Notes

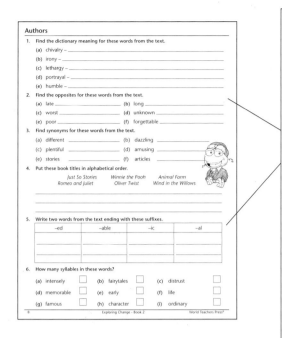

Page Three provides a variety of word study activities. The words used are either from the text, or the answer can be found in the text.

Words common to the text can be used to develop skills in other areas of language development. Word study activities can be used to aid students in their understanding of text and the way it works, as well as improving general spelling.

Introduce the word study skill through discussion and encourage students to share their knowledge with their peers.

Explain and provide clear examples of the word study skill to be covered to ensure students have a full understanding before completing the worksheet.

Read through the questions on the worksheet and demonstrate how to complete them appropriately. Students then complete the activity. Worksheets can be collected to ascertain students' understanding.

Page Four contains a variety of creative activities. The curriculum areas vary from topic to topic and include studies of Society and Culture, Science, Mathematics, English and Technology.

Each activity can be used as a follow-up activity to provide students with the opportunity to develop and practice skills in other areas outside language.

Completed activities can be displayed in the classroom with an overview sheet made by the students outlining what they have learned about the topic.

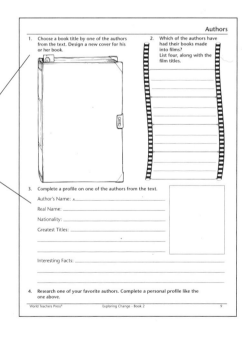

Exploring Change – Grades 5–6 can be treated separately as part of Studies of Society and Culture or thematically over several key learning areas.

The activities may be compiled into topic booklets, theme booklets, a file, or scrapbook.

Activities can also be used as homework projects.

Another alternative could be for small groups of students to complete different topics. Students' work can be displayed for others to view after a report has been presented to the rest of the class.

Authors

Wolfram von Eschenbach (1170–1220)
This German poet is also a knight. He leads a roving life, and his only completed work is *Parzival* (*Parsifal*), a humorous poem of chivalry. Richard Wagner's opera *Parsifal* is based on this work.

Geoffrey Chaucer (1343–1400)
From humble beginnings, Chaucer becomes the first great English poet. Influenced by French and Italian writers, his greatest work is *The Canterbury Tales*. He dies before it is complete and is buried in Westminster Abbey.

Sir Thomas More (1478–1535)
Born in London, Thomas More soon shows himself to be a great scholar and a devoutly religious man. He writes many different works, but his best known is *Utopia*. Once a friend of King Henry VII, he falls from favor and is executed for treason. In 1935, he is named a Saint.

William Shakespeare (1564–1616)

Shakespeare is possibly the most famous of all British dramatists and poets. His work is still studied and performed today. Among his more well-known titles are *Hamlet*, *Macbeth*, *Romeo and Juliet* and *A Midsummer Night's Dream*.

Daniel Defoe (1660–1731)
From an early age, this English author writes many political essays and pamphlets. He is best known for his novel called (in full) *The Life and Strange and Surprising Adventures of Robinson Crusoe, of York, Mariner*. He dies, it is said, of "lethargy."

Jane Austen (1775–1817)
This English writer is noted for her light irony, humor and witty depiction of country life, with its underlying seriousness. Her famous titles include *Pride and Prejudice*, *Emma* and *Sense and Sensibility*.

Hans Christian Andersen (1805–1875)
A prolific Danish author, Andersen has some 168 folktales and fairytales published, especially for children. His best-known titles include *The Ugly Duckling*, *The Little Mermaid* and *Hansel and Gretel*.

Charles Dickens (1812–1870)
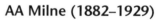
This English author, with a huge list of books to his credit, is best known for his rich and varied portrayal of society of his times. Among his titles are *Oliver Twist*, *A Tale of Two Cities*, *A Christmas Carol* and *Great Expectations*.

Lewis Carroll (1832–1898)

His real name is the Rev. Charles Lutwidge Dodgson. He is an intensely shy man, but also a brilliant mathematician. He sometimes says his only friends are children. Two of his best known titles are *Alice's Adventures in Wonderland* and *Through the Looking Glass*.

Mark Twain (1835–1910)
Samuel Langhorne Clemens (his real name) writes of ordinary people and draws a realistic picture of 19th century life. He is best known for *The Prince and the Pauper*, *The Adventures of Tom Sawyer* and *The Adventures of Huckleberry Finn*.

Andrew Barton ("Banjo") Paterson (1864–1941)
Banjo Paterson is one of Australia's first great literary figures. A journalist, he writes of the Australian Outback in such memorable poems as *Clancy of the Overflow*, *Waltzing Matilda* and *The Man from Snowy River*.

Rudyard Kipling (1865–1936)
Rudyard Kipling is born in India, but is sent back to England as a child, which makes him very unhappy. As an adult, he goes to live in America, where he writes *The Jungle Book*, published in 1894. In 1901 comes *Kim* and in 1902, the *Just So Stories*. In 1907, he is the first English writer to be awarded the Nobel Prize.

Henry Lawson (1867–1922)
Best known as "the people's poet," Lawson uses the Australian bush and its people for his short stories and dozens of poems. He is said to be the first to capture the spirit of the Australian way of life. His works include *The Loaded Dog* and *The Drover's Wife*.

AA Milne (1882–1929)
Famous children's author who created many outstanding and unforgettable characters, including Pooh Bear, Tigger and Eeyore (*Winnie-the-Pooh*), and Toad of Toad Hall (*Wind in the Willows*).

George Orwell (1903–1950)

This British author (real name Eric Blair) has a lifelong distrust of totalitarian governments. Although he writes documentaries and essays and is a critic, he is possibly best known for two titles: *Animal Farm* and *1984*.

Authors

Use the text to answer these questions.

1. **Name a book title written by these authors.**

    (a) George Orwell _____

    (b) Geoffrey Chaucer _____

    (c) Rudyard Kipling _____

    (d) William Shakespeare _____

    (e) Charles Dickens _____

2. _____ won a Nobel Prize in _____.

3. **What settings did these writers favor for their work?**

    (a) Henry Lawson _____

    (b) Jane Austen _____

    (c) Banjo Paterson _____

    (d) Mark Twain _____

4. **Name three characters developed by AA Milne.**

    _____

    _____

5. **Who was once a friend of King Henry VII? Explain what happened to him.**

    _____

    _____

6. **Complete the table with names from the text.**

English Poets	Children's Authors	Australian Authors

7. **Under what other name did these writers become famous?**

    (a) Rev. Charles Lutwidge Dodgson _____

    (b) Eric Blair _____

    (c) Samuel Langhorne Clemens _____

    (d) Andrew Barton Paterson _____

Authors

1. Find the dictionary meaning for these words from the text.
   - (a) chivalry – _____
   - (b) irony – _____
   - (c) lethargy – _____
   - (d) portrayal – _____
   - (e) humble – _____

2. Find the opposites for these words from the text.
   - (a) late _____
   - (b) long _____
   - (c) worst _____
   - (d) unknown _____
   - (e) poor _____
   - (f) forgettable _____

3. Find synonyms for these words from the text.
   - (a) different _____
   - (b) dazzling _____
   - (c) plentiful _____
   - (d) amusing _____
   - (e) stories _____
   - (f) articles _____

4. Put these book titles in alphabetical order.

   Just So Stories   *Winnie-the-Pooh*   *Animal Farm*
   Romeo and Juliet   *Oliver Twist*   *Wind in the Willows*

   _____
   _____
   _____

5. Write two words from the text ending with these suffixes.

–ed	–able	–ic	–al

6. How many syllables in these words?
   - (a) intensely ☐
   - (b) fairytales ☐
   - (c) distrust ☐
   - (d) memorable ☐
   - (e) early ☐
   - (f) life ☐
   - (g) famous ☐
   - (h) character ☐
   - (i) ordinary ☐

Authors

1. Choose a book title by one of the authors from the text. Design a new cover for his or her book.

2. Which of the authors have had their books made into films?
   List four, along with the film titles.

3. Complete a profile on one of the authors from the text.

   Author's Name: _____

   Real Name: _____

   Nationality: _____

   Greatest Titles: _____

   _____

   Interesting Facts: _____

   _____

4. Research one of your favorite authors. Complete a personal profile like the one above.

World Teachers Press® — Exploring Change - Book 2

Clothing

At first, clothes are worn for protection. As time goes by, clothing is used for modesty and fashion purposes. Different societies change their way of dressing through the millennium. Changing lifestyles and fashions affect the clothes people wear.

Here is how fashions change in Europe through the millennium.

1000 – 1500

As society leaves the Dark Ages, life slowly but steadily gets better for most people. This shows in the clothes people wear. Arts and crafts begin to flourish, and people also start to dress with greater care.

Ordinary people wear rough woolen breeches. Those worn by the rich are made of silk.

At home, women wear a simple tunic. They add a robe and hooded cloak when they go out.

A lord's tunic and cloak become longer and more colorful.

Fashionable women wear gowns with long, hanging sleeves.

1500 – 1850

Increasing trade with other countries in the world sees many new skills and ideas introduced in the clothing and textile industries.

Between 1500 and 1700, clothes become more decorative. Hats, bags and jewelry are added.

Lace is very popular in Holland. It is worn mainly on collars and cuffs.

From 1700 to 1900 clothes gradually become simpler. The jacket, waistcoat and trousers are introduced.

1850 – 2000

The sewing machine is invented and more and more clothes are mass-produced. Stores begin selling ready-made clothes.

Workers begin to wear specially-designed uniforms.

By the 1930s, women are wearing shorter dresses during the days, and men's suits are less "fussy."

Since the 1950s, artificial fibers have made clothes cheap, comfortable and easy to clean.

Clothing

Use the text to answer these questions.

1. **List three reasons why people wear clothing.**
   _____
   _____
   _____

2. **Why have people changed their way of dressing over the millennium?**
   _____
   _____
   _____

3. **Answer true or false.**

    (a) Life was easy in the Dark Ages. _____

    (b) Rich people wore breeches of silk. _____

    (c) Hats, bags and jewelry became popular after 1500. _____

    (d) Clothes are easier to clean now. _____

    (e) People dressed with greater care before 1000. _____

    (f) Stores sold ready-made clothes in 1750. _____

4. **Do you think the sewing machine was an important invention?**
   _____ Why/Why not? _____
   _____
   _____

5. **What effect did increasing trade with other countries have on the clothing industry?**
   _____
   _____
   _____

6. **Describe clothes in the 1930s.**
   _____
   _____
   _____

7. **Over the past 150 years people have begun to wear specially-designed uniforms. Draw, color and label a uniform on a separate piece of paper.**

Clothing

1. Find the dictionary meaning for the following words.
   - (a) modesty _____
   - (b) textile _____
   - (c) mass-produced _____
   - (d) artificial _____
   - (e) fibers _____

2. Write an article of clothing—modern or from the past—for each letter below.

   c_____
   p_____
   t_____
   h_____
   s_____ r_____
   b_____ w_____
   d_____ j_____

3. Write a word from the text ending with these suffixes. Then write one of your own.

-ed	-ing	-able	-er	-ive

4. Find a synonym for these words from the text.
   - (a) easier _____
   - (b) cover _____
   - (c) pants _____
   - (d) thrive _____
   - (e) concern _____
   - (f) ornamental _____

5. Put the apostrophe in the correct place. For example, men's suits.
   - (a) childrens clothes
   - (b) a ladys hat
   - (c) the boys shirt
   - (d) a lords tunic
   - (e) the girls dress
   - (f) ladies bags
   - (g) womens shoes
   - (h) a workers uniform
   - (i) mens trousers
   - (j) a childs coat

Clothing

1. Study the three pictures below. Decide which clothes would be worn by people between 1000 – 1500, 1500 – 1850, 1850 – today.
   Label each picture and give a reason for your choice.

   (a) Between _____
   _____
   _____
   _____
   _____

   (b) Between _____
   _____
   _____
   _____
   _____

   (c) Between _____
   _____
   _____
   _____
   _____

2. Choose two of the fashions above. Circle your choices (a), (b) or (c).
   List the similarities and differences you notice in each.

Similarities	Differences

World Teachers Press®   Exploring Change - Book 2

Communication

Before they even spoke actual words, early humans communicated through sounds and gestures. Paintings and drawings were the first steps towards a written language before printing was eventually developed.

Around the year 1000, printed books are found in China. The printers put ink on engraved wooden blocks and press them against paper. In Europe, information is still being spread by word of mouth, or written out by hand.

Playing cards

The earliest use of printing in Europe is to make cards, not books. When playing cards are first introduced in Europe in the mid-1300s, they are hand drawn. However, printers soon learn to print cards using "block printing," which is similar to the Chinese method.

Gutenberg's Press

Johannes Gutenberg, a German metalsmith, invents the first printing press in Europe in 1454. He casts individual raised metal letters and coats them with an oily ink. The letters are then stamped onto paper with a screw press. Now books can be produced quickly and easily, but they are still very expensive.

First Pencils

In the mid 1500s, the English make the first pencils to use graphite, the "lead" that is still used today.

First Office Copier

James Watt is most famous for developing the steam engine. However, between 1777 and 1780, he also invents the first office copier. Not everyone is impressed as some think the machine will encourage forgery.

Steam-powered Printing Press

In 1811, Frederick König invents a steam-powered press which greatly speeds up printing. König continues to improve his press and creates one which prints both sides of a sheet of paper at once.

Shorthand

This is a method of writing rapidly by using symbols or letters to represent the sounds of words. The most widely used system is invented in 1837 by Isaac Pitman.

Typewriter

When typewriters are first invented, typists can jam them by typing too quickly. In 1874, an American inventor named Christopher Sholes solves this by redesigning the keyboard layout, making it easier to type quickly. This is the "qwerty" keyboard still in use today.

Ballpoint Pens

Until 1830, quills (made from goose feathers) were the standard pens. These are replaced by steel "nibs." It isn't until the late 1930s that Ladislo Biro's ballpoint pen is widely used.

Photocopier

Electrostatic photocopying (xerography) is invented in 1938 by an American, Chester F. Carlson. This process revolutionizes offices and the copying industry.

Word Processor

The first word processors appear in the 1960s and rapidly take over for typewriters. They have become smaller, faster and cheaper since then.

Laser Printers

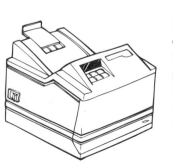

In the mid-1980s, desktop computers and laser printers lead to a revolution in the printing and publishing industries. They are now the most common form of printing.

Communication

Use the text to answer these questions.

1. **How was information spread in Europe around the year 1000?**

   _____

   _____

2. **Check the correct answers.**

   (a) Quill pens were made of…

   ☐ duck feathers.
   ☐ goose feathers.
   ☐ chicken feathers.

   (b) James Watt was most famous for…

   ☐ inventing the typewriter.
   ☐ inventing the office copier.
   ☐ developing the steam engine.

3. **Complete the cloze about Johannes Gutenberg's invention.**

   Johannes _____, who invented the first _____ _____ in 1454, was a _____ metalsmith. He casts individual raised _____ letters and _____ them with an _____ ink. The _____ are then stamped onto _____ with a screw press.

   Although _____ can now be produced more _____ and _____ they are still very _____.

4. **When typewriters were first invented, typists often jammed them. How was this problem solved?**

   _____

   _____

   _____

   _____

5. **What invention took over for…**

   (a) the typewriter?

   _____

   (b) the office copier?

   _____

6. **Briefly describe Isaac Pitman's invention.**

   _____

   _____

   _____

Communication

1. Homophones are words that sound the same but which have different spellings and meanings. Find homophones in the text for these.

    (a) witch _____   (b) to _____

    (c) knot _____   (d) led _____

    (e) steal _____   (f) threw _____

2. Complete the table below with words from the text. Use each word only once.

Three syllables	Noun	Verb	Compound word

3. Find the dictionary meaning for the following words.

    (a) forgery _____

    (b) engraved _____

    (c) gestures _____

    (d) graphite _____

4. Write a rhyming word from the text for each of these.

    (a) corn _____   (b) yards _____

    (c) blink _____   (d) baking _____

    (e) south _____   (f) beam _____

5. Find small words in these.

    (a) replaced _____

    (b) drawings _____

    (c) typewriters _____

6. Can you find a word with six syllables in the text?

    _____

Communication

1. Use the numbers 1 – 12 to order these inventions or developments in communication.

   ☐ The first pencils to use graphite are made.
   ☐ The first office copier is invented.
   ☐ Desktop computers and laser printers revolutionize the printing and publishing industry.
   ☐ Playing cards appear in Europe.
   ☐ The system of shorthand is invented.
   ☐ The steam-powered press greatly speeds up printing.

   ☐ First word processors appear.
   ☐ Printed books are used in China.
   ☐ Electrostatic photocopying is invented.
   ☐ The first printing press is invented.
   ☐ Typewriters are invented.
   ☐ Ladislo Biro's ballpoint pen is widely used.

2. **Card games have been popular throughout the millennium. List as many as you can. Compare with a friend.**

   _____
   _____
   _____
   _____

3. Complete the communication quiz. (Try not to use the text.)

   (a) Books were cheap in the 1500s.   ☐ true   ☐ false
   (b) The "qwerty" keyboard layout is still used.   ☐ true   ☐ false
   (c) König's press printed one side only.   ☐ true   ☐ false
   (d) Laser printers are uncommon.   ☐ true   ☐ false
   (e) Who invented the electrostatic photocopier? _____
   (f) Name three communication inventions of the 20th Century described in the text.
       _____ _____ _____
   (g) Which two people invented or improved the printing press?
       _____
       _____

Score /10

Cooking

Before stoves and microwave ovens, fire was used for cooking. By the turn of the millennium, people had developed a good understanding of the use of heat in cooking. Most kitchens had brick ovens and earthenware was used for cooking meals. Cooking remained more or less the same until the 1700s, when it evolved, quite quickly, into what we know today.

400s–1500s

During the Middle Ages, Europeans use fireplaces for cooking. People either heat food in a kettle or broil meat on a spit. Many European towns have public ovens for people to use, as a lot of people do not have an oven in their home.

1600s–1700s

The people of North America also cook their food in kettles or on spits in their fireplace during the 1600s and 1700s. Many fireplaces have built-in ovens. During the 1800s, iron cookstoves, which burn wood, become popular.

French scientist, Denis Papin, invents the first pressure cooker in London in 1680. This invention is welcomed because it greatly reduces cooking time.

1700s–1800s

In 1784, the Germans develop a wood-fired stove which has a spit to turn meat and a hood to take away the smoke. The removal of smoke from the cooking place is greatly appreciated as it makes breathing easier for those working in the kitchen.

In 1855, Robert Bunsen, a German chemist, invents the first practical gas burner. In the 1860s, gas cookers become popular in cities that have gas piped into homes. Gas burners are not popular in country areas until 1910, when gas can be shipped out to country homes in cylinders.

1900s

Electric cookers are first sold in 1909. Because these early cookers are extremely slow, they are not very popular. By 1930, electric cookers have been improved to make cooking faster, which increases their popularity.

In 1937, the first commercial microwave oven is available. It is invented by Dr. Percy Spencer and is almost 1.68 meters tall and weighs more than 340 kg. Each microwave oven costs about $5,000.

By 1976, microwave ovens are becoming common in modern kitchens. The microwave oven works by using radio waves that penetrate the food and vibrate its molecules. The friction among the moving molecules produces heat, which cooks the food. Due to their cost they were once considered a luxury. Today, they are considered a necessity in our fast-paced lifestyle.

By the early 1980s, convection, or hot-air, ovens are becoming popular. This type of oven is available in gas and electric models. The convection oven relies on blowers which circulate the hot air around the food. This means the oven cooks food faster and more evenly, at a lower temperature. Using lower temperatures means costs are kept down, as less gas or electricity is used.

Thanks to the continuing development of cooking appliances over the past two hundred years, cooking is now easier and faster than ever before.

Cooking

Use the text to answer these questions.

1. **Write the dates for the following events.**

    (a) The first microwave oven became available. _____

    (b) Gas cookers became popular in country areas. _____

    (c) Electric cookers were first sold. _____

    (d) Convection ovens became popular. _____

2. **Name the inventor of each of these products.**

    (a) Pressure cooker _____

    (b) Gas cooker _____

    (c) Microwave oven _____

3. **Write "fact" or "opinion" beside each of these statements.**

    (a) Every home should have a microwave oven. _____

    (b) The convection oven is the best oven money can buy. _____

    (c) Convection ovens cook food faster than regular ovens. _____

    (d) Pressure cookers reduce cooking time. _____

4. **How did the people of North America cook their food during the 1600s and 1700s?**

    _____

5. **Explain how a microwave oven cooks food.**

    _____

    _____

6. **Explain why you think there weren't many developments in cooking until the 1700s.**

    _____

    _____

7. **Discuss how you think cooking will develop further in the future.**

    _____

    _____

    _____

Cooking

1. Write these words in alphabetical order.

    oven   fireplace   cooker   gas   electric   microwave   convection

    _____

    _____

2. Find the meaning of these words.

    (a) molecules _____

    (b) vibrate _____

    (c) friction _____

    (d) penetrate _____

    (e) practical _____

    (f) circulate _____

3. Complete this table.

    Write a word from the text with these letter patterns, then write one word of your own. Each word needs to make a long "a" sound.

a–e	ay	ey	eigh	ai

4. Find hidden words within these words.

    For example; from heat we can make *he, at* and *eat*.

    (a) penetrate _____

    (b) fireplaces _____

    (c) invention _____

    (d) understanding _____

5. Write anagrams for these words.

    An anagram is a word made from the letters of another word.

    For example; *its* can be rearranged to make *sit*.

    (a) meat _____

    (b) time _____

    (c) was _____

    (d) gas _____

Cooking

1. **Design an oven that could be used in the new millennium.**
   Remember to include materials, power source (gas, electric, solar-powered, or wind-powered).
   Draw your design, label each part and explain how it is used.

   _____
   _____
   _____
   _____
   _____
   _____
   _____
   _____

2. **Design a brochure to advertise your new oven.**
   Plan it below. Remember to use bright colors and to include all of its strengths as well as the cost.

3. **Imagine you are in a forest. You are very hungry and happen across some sweet potatoes. You cannot eat them raw and need to cook them. You have no cooking equipment with you. How are you going to cook them?**

   On a separate piece of paper, draw a flow chart to show what you will do. Label and explain each stage of the procedure.

Energy

Before the Millennium

Before this millennium, the most common forms of energy are the sun, human muscles, fire, animal power, animal dung, charcoal, coal, animal oils, water power and wind power.

1698

Thomas Savery is the first to harness the power of steam in a practical way. He invents a steam-powered pump to draw water up from mines in south-west England. This is later improved on by Thomas Newcomen. The steam engine becomes the chief energy form for industry and transportation during the Industrial Revolution.

1709

In the 1600s, a shortage of wood has made charcoal very expensive in England. English ironworkers heat coal in brick ovens to remove impurities. They use the "cooked" coal—called coke—to burn as an energy source.

1815

It is discovered that, when heating coal, a flammable gas is given off. It takes some time to discover a way to collect and distribute this gas.

1859

Large-scale oil drilling begins when Edwin Drake, an American, drills the first oil well in Pennsylvania. Oil drilling soon becomes a major industry in America.

1873

Electricity is first generated using dynamos developed by Zénobe Gramme. The electricity is used to power factories, machinery and household appliances.

1881

The first hydroelectric power plant comes into operation in England. This produces electricity by directing running water to turn turbines.

1904

It is discovered that "geothermal energy," heat from the Earth itself, can be used as a power source. The first plant, in Italy, begins generating electricity using steam expelled from volcanic holes.

1942

The first nuclear reactor is built from an idea developed by an Italian-American physicist, Enrico Fermi. He wants to prove that nuclear energy is a source of endless, non-polluting power.

1945

Drilling rigs for oil are set up on the seabed off the American coast. Until now, petroleum gas, always found with oil, has been burned off on the oil rig. Now, however, the value of the gas is realized and it is transported to shore for use.

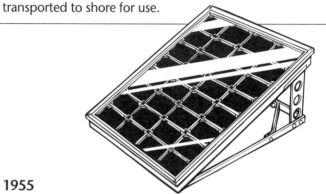

1955

Solar cells are used to generate power directly from the sun. Although expensive, solar energy panels are able to contribute useful amounts of energy for use by households. Solar power provides a clean and almost unlimited energy source. However, darkness and overcast weather interrupt the power output.

1966

The idea of using waves and tides to produce energy is put forward. It is still in the developmental stages today. The disadvantages are that tidal power plants only work on a falling tide, and they can only be built in a few places which have sufficiently large tides.

1975

Although alcohol has been used as fuel before, it isn't until Brazil produces alcohol from sugar cane that it is used as a fuel for motor vehicles. The problem is that it takes as much energy to produce the fuel as the fuel makes when it is burned in an engine.

1982

Wind power is first used commercially in Washington. Wind "farms" produce enough power for hundreds of homes. However, the farms need a lot of room, and the "windmills" are very noisy. And, of course, they are only practical where there are strong, steady winds.

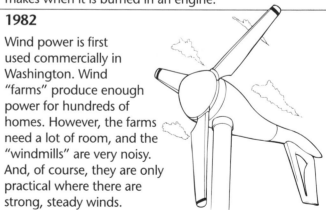

1990s

Fusion reactors are under development. These work on the principle of forcing atoms together at extremely high temperatures to release energy. This may be the most efficient form of energy production to date.

Energy

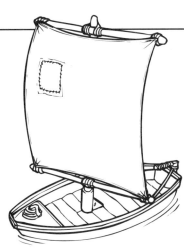

Use the text to answer these questions.

1. List four important sources of energy used before this millennium.
   _____
   _____
   _____
   _____

2. Who first used steam power and for what use?
   _____

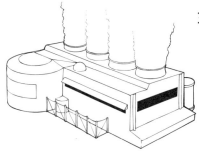

3. Explain the term "geothermal energy."
   _____
   _____
   _____
   _____

4. List items that use these forms of energy.
   (a) electric – _____
   (b) gas – _____
   (c) wind – _____
   (d) solar – _____

5. Match the energy terms with their meanings.

   (a) hydroelectric power • • heat from the earth used as a power source

   (b) fusion • • once called dynamos, they generate the power for most electrical sources

   (c) geothermal energy • • convert sunlight directly into electricity

   (d) electric generators • • electricity generated from falling or running water

   (e) solar cells • • forcing atoms to release energy by exposing them to extreme heat

6. Which energy source is the most commonly used? Give reasons for your answer.
   _____
   _____
   _____

Energy

1. Write word builders for these words from the text.

    (a) power _____

    (b) generate _____

    (c) use _____

    (d) produce _____

2. Put these words into alphabetical order

    gas	given	geothermal	great	generate	go

    _____

    _____

3. Find the opposite of these words in the text.

    (a) quiet _____ (b) never _____

    (c) capture _____ (d) inefficient _____

    (e) last _____ (f) after _____

4. Compound words are two words joined to make a new word (for example, sunshine). Find two compound words from the text and write four more of your own.

    _____ _____ _____

    _____ _____ _____

5. Homographs are words that are spelled the same but that have different meanings. Find two meanings for these homographs.

    down – _____

    _____

    _____

    power – _____

    _____

    drill – _____

    _____

6. Find words from the text to complete the table using these prefixes.

re	dis	be

Energy

1. **Electricity has made our lives much easier and more enjoyable. Complete the list below with electrical items that you see or use.**

    At home

    sewing machine, _____
    _____
    _____
    _____

    At school

    computer, _____
    _____
    _____
    _____

3. **Give advantages and disadvantages for these power sources.**

	Advantages	Disadvantages
Solar		
Wind		

    Extra: Find out what these people have to do with electricity—Thomas Edison, Alessandra Volta, Michael Faraday.

2. **Complete the timeline with information from the text.**

    1698 — T. Savery invents a _____ pump for mines.

    1709 — Wood shortage made _____ very expensive.

    1815 — Heating coal produces flammable gas.

    1859 — _____

    1873 — first generated using _____.

    1881 — First _____ power.

    1904 — Electricity produced from _____.

    1942 — First nuclear reactor built.

    1945 — _____ transported to shore.

    1955 — generate power from the _____.

    1966 — Tidal power plants developing.

    1975 — produced from _____.

    1982 — first used commercially in _____.

    1990s — _____ used to fuel _____.

    reactors under development.

World Teachers Press® — Exploring Change - Book 2

Farming

Before the Millennium

Some animals, such as sheep and goats, have been domesticated. Others, such as dogs, have been trained to work with people. Farming encourages people to settle and stay in one area.

A basic plow pulled by oxen is used to make farming easier.

Bulls are raised to pull carts or for beef.

1000s

People are not able to gather enough food to feed their stock over winter. Older animals are generally slaughtered and their meat salted or dried. Wheeled carts are used instead of sleds on "skids."

1573

The potato is introduced to Europe from America. It quickly becomes a staple food.

A few years later, the tomato is introduced from Mexico.

1701

Jethro Tull's invention, the "seed drill," allows grain to be planted in rows, using less seed.

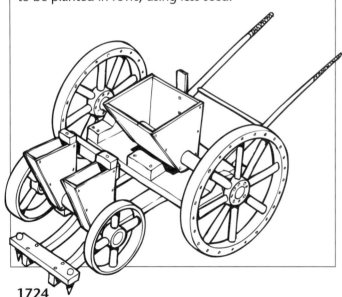

1724

English farmers begin to grow turnips for food over winter. This means fewer stock are slaughtered, as there is now enough feed. But farmers work hard for long hours to produce scant crops.

1745

Robert Bakewell discovers that only allowing the best stock to breed improves the quality of their offspring. William Ellis invents a drill plow, allowing seed to be dropped directly as the soil is plowed.

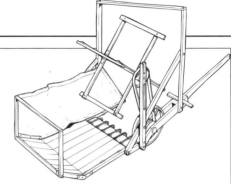

1831

A farmer named McCormick invents a horse-drawn reaper (harvesting machine). This has cutting knives along one side and is pulled in rows up and down the field to cut the crop. It allows a farmer to harvest four or five times as much grain a day as before.

1837

John Deere introduces the first all-steel plow. This is much stronger than the plows then in use.

Mid-1800s

Andrew Meikle invents a machine that makes threshing (separating the grain) easier.

1930s

The "combine harvester" is introduced. This machine reaps, threshes, stores the grain and makes hay bales while crossing the field.

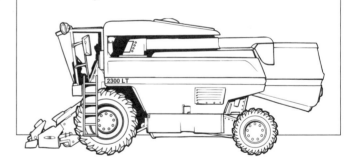

Today

In 1700, it took 90% of the world's population to produce 100% of the food required.

Today, it takes only 3% of the world's population to produce 120% of the food required. (The surplus food is stored.)

Irrigation develops over the millennium from using buckets to hand-operated pumps to huge sprinkler systems which can move across the fields under their own power.

A greater use of fertilizer and pesticides has had negative effects on the environment. There is a growing trend for "organic" food crops, which use no chemicals.

Farming

Use the text to answer these questions.

1. What uses did animals have in early farming?
   _____
   _____
   _____

2. What did English farmers begin to grow in the 1700s to ensure there was enough food for winter?

   tomatoes   potatoes   corn   turnips

3. Explain the jobs done by a combine harvester.
   _____
   _____
   _____

4. List three changes in irrigation through the millennium.
   _____
   _____
   _____

5. True or False

   (a) The horse-drawn reaper is pulled in rows to cut crops. ☐ true ☐ false

   (b) The tomato was introduced to America from Europe. ☐ true ☐ false

   (c) Wheels are added to carts at the beginning of the millennium. ☐ true ☐ false

   (d) Bulls were raised to pull carts or for beef. ☐ true ☐ false

   (e) Organic food crops use lots of chemicals. ☐ true ☐ false

   (f) The drill plow drops seeds directly into the plowed soil. ☐ true ☐ false

6. Which invention do you think was most important in farming history? Give reasons.
   _____
   _____
   _____
   _____

Farming

1. **Unjumble this information from the text.**

   (a) dried is Meat animals or salted. slaughtered from

   _____

   (b) be drill planted grain The rows. in allows to seed

   _____

2. **Write the plural of these words. Take care with your spelling.**

   (a) tomato _____   (b) grain _____

   (c) turnip _____   (d) potato _____

   (e) knife _____   (f) chemical _____

   (g) child _____   (h) sheep _____

3. **Write the antonym for each word in bold print to make new phrases.**

   (a) **huge** sprinkler systems _____

   (b) carts **harder** to move _____

   (c) **slowly** becomes a staple food _____

   (d) **negative** effects on the environment _____

4. **Find a rhyming word from the text.**

   (a) shoulder _____   (b) feet _____

   (c) read _____   (d) sails _____

   (e) cows _____   (f) blend _____

5. **Use a dictionary to help you find word builders for these.**

   (a) mean – _____

   (b) plant – _____

   (c) seed – _____

   (d) invent – _____

6. **Complete the table with words from the text with these letter patterns.**

–ee	–ow	–tion	–er

Farming

1. Choose a title for each picture. Write an important fact or facts about each farming method.

   | Jethro Tull Seed Drill | Modern Irrigation System | McCormick's Reaper Machine | Combine Harvester |

   (a) _____

   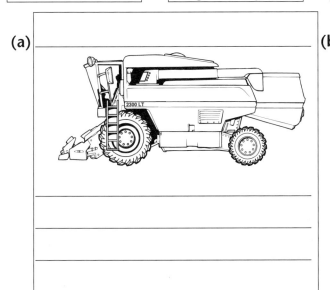

   _____
   _____
   _____
   _____

   (b) _____

   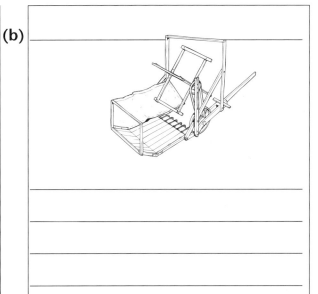

   _____
   _____
   _____
   _____

   (c) _____

   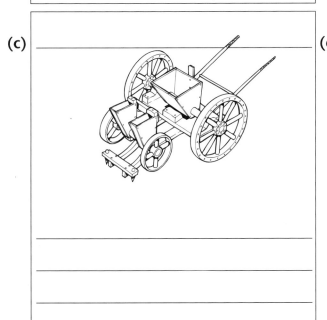

   _____
   _____
   _____
   _____

   (d) _____

   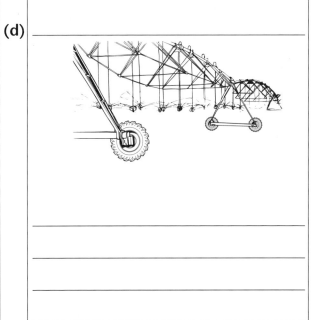

   _____
   _____
   _____
   _____

2. Can you find fifteen farming or food words hidden in the word search? List them.

H	I	R	R	I	G	A	T	I	O	N	P
S	H	F	E	R	T	I	L	I	Z	E	R
L	A	A	A	G	R	A	I	N	D	Y	O
A	R	R	P	L	A	P	L	O	W	G	H
M	V	M	E	B	C	M	D	E	E	S	A
I	E	E	R	E	T	S	T	O	C	K	Y
N	S	R	R	E	O	P	I	N	R	U	T
A	T	S	G	F	R	L	L	I	R	D	N

   _____
   _____
   _____
   _____
   _____
   _____
   _____

Medicine

Before the Millennium

Ancient physicians are surprisingly skilled, carrying out a form of brain surgery, acupuncture and even plastic surgery. However, after the fall of the Greek and Roman Empires, European medicine goes into a serious decline. Much of what was known in earlier times is lost. Medicine is often practiced with magic, witchcraft and astrology. Seriously ill patients rarely survive!

1500s

Andreas Vesalius, a Belgian physician, dissects human bodies to learn more about anatomy. His work shows that much of what is believed about the body is not true, because it is based on animal anatomy.

Theophrastus Phillipus Aureolus Bombastus von Hohenheim (also known as Paracelsus) writes the first textbook on surgery. He also correctly decides that diseases are caused by something outside the body—something like what we now call bacteria.

1628

An English doctor, William Harvey, shows how the heart and blood vessels work to circulate blood through the body.

1753

Sailors on long voyages suffer from a disease called scurvy. Physician James Lind discovers it is caused by a vitamin C deficiency, and suggests lime juice as a cure.

1796

Edward Jenner discovers the medical procedure called inoculation. He deliberately infects a boy with cowpox, which gives him a resistance to the more serious disease smallpox.

1800s

Louis Pasteur improves Jenner's work, developing the process called vaccination. He proves that infecting a person with a mild form of a disease prevents that person from suffering a severe attack of the same disease.

1846

Until now, operations are usually performed on patients while they are still awake! William Morten, an American dentist, uses ether to put patients to sleep during surgery.

1856

Joseph Lister makes surgery a much safer practice by using carbolic acid to clean instruments and dressings, killing germs.

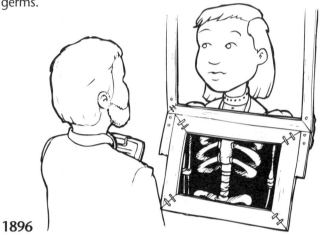

1896

Wilhelm Conrad Röntgen, a German physicist, discovers Röntgen rays, or X-rays, allowing doctors to "see" inside a living body.

1928

A Scottish scientist, Alexander Fleming, discovers penicillin, an antibiotic that has been called the greatest medical discovery so far.

1953

The structure of our "genetic code," called DNA, is uncovered by two British scientists, James Watson and Francis Crick.

An American doctor, John Gibbon, invents the heart-lung machine, which allows major heart surgery to become a reality.

1967

The first heart transplant is carried out in South Africa. The surgeon is Dr. Christiaan Barnard.

1970 – 1980

"Scanning" the brain to produce a 3-D image is a huge step forward in combating brain disorders.

1980 – 1990

The development of microsurgery means that parts inside the human body too small to be seen with the naked eye can now be operated on.

1990s

Ultrasound technology gives doctors another, safer tool to look inside the human body.

Medicine

Use the text to answer these questions.

1. What important contributions did these people make to medicine?

    (a) Joseph Lister – _____

    _____

    (b) William Harvey – _____

    _____

    (c) Louis Pasteur – _____

    _____

    (d) Wilhelm Conrad Röntgen – _____

    _____

2. How has "microsurgery" improved medical procedures?

    _____
    _____
    _____

3. How were patients treated after the fall of the Roman and Greek Empires?

    _____
    _____
    _____

4. Why do you think Alexander Fleming's discovery was so important to medical history?

    _____
    _____

5. How could scurvy be cured?

    _____
    _____

6. Match the medical discoveries with their discoverer and the date.

Ether •	• Dr. Christiaan Barnard •	• 1967
Human anatomy •	• Edward Jenner •	• 1953
First heart transplant •	• Andreas Vesalius •	• 1628
Blood circulation •	• William Morten •	• 1500s
Inoculation •	• Dr. John Gibbon •	• 1846
Heart-lung machine •	• William Harvey •	• 1796

7. Which discovery do you think was most important to us? Give reasons why.

    _____
    _____

Medicine

1. **Find the meaning of these "medicine" words.**

   (a) antibiotic – _____

   (b) penicillin – _____

   (c) bacteria – _____

   (d) ultrasound – _____

2. **Find hidden words within these words.**

   (a) instruments _____

   (b) performed _____

   (c) something _____

   (d) smallpox _____

3. **Complete the table below.**

		greatest
early		
	smaller	
		rarest
mean		
	milder	

4. **Put these words into alphabetical order.**

   genetic, scanning, scurvy, resistance, doctor, safer, brain, vaccination, disease

   _____

   _____

5. **Write the number of syllables for each word.**

   (a) technology ☐   (b) ultrasound ☐   (c) heart ☐

   (d) scurvy ☐   (e) physicist ☐   (f) astrology ☐

   (g) development ☐   (h) disease ☐   (i) germs ☐

   (j) anatomy ☐   (k) body ☐   (l) vaccination ☐

6. **Unjumble this information from the text.**

   (a) body. vessels the Blood blood circulate through

   _____

   (b) instruments Carbolic and clean used dressings. is to acid

   _____

Medicine

1. **Choose one of the developments in medicine. Imagine you are a reporter getting the "scoop" on this discovery. Plan your story under the headings below.**

   Who...   What...   When...
   _____   _____   _____
   _____   _____   _____
   _____   _____   _____
   _____   _____   _____

   Where...   Why...   Conclusion
   _____   _____   _____
   _____   _____   _____
   _____   _____   _____
   _____   _____   _____

   Make a headline for your story.

   ```
   $1.50          ◆ THE NEWS TODAY ◆          Date: _____
   ```

2. **Design a health poster to promote how cleanliness can keep germs and disease at bay. Use the space below to plan your notes and artwork before doing a final copy.**

Notes:	Art Ideas...
Wash hands before eating.	

Sea Exploration

At the beginning of the millennium, people know very little about what exists more than a few days' journey from where they live. Even up until the 1400s, most people see the world as a "small" place, stretching no further than the next town or village. They do not know that whole countries and civilizations exist beyond their own.

From around 1450, however, European sailors and navigators set out on remarkable voyages of exploration. They are driven by curiosity and the search for trade to add to their countries' wealth. Continuing developments in ship construction and navigation from this time enabled these adventurers to travel further into the unknown.

Christopher Columbus

In 1492, Christopher Columbus, an Italian, is given a small fleet by the Spanish to find new trade routes to India. Instead, he finds a group of islands which he calls the West Indies, believing them to be part of India. Columbus also makes three more voyages to the region.

Dirk Hartog

Dirk Hartog, a Dutch explorer, is the first European to land on the western coast of Australia. He marks his arrival in 1616 by nailing an inscribed pewter plate to a post. Hartog is sailing to the Dutch East Indies (Indonesia) when he sails too far east and sights land, now known as Dirk Hartog Island.

Vasco da Gama

In 1498, da Gama, a Portuguese explorer, becomes the first European to make a sea voyage to India from Europe by sailing around Africa. This voyage opens up the first all-water trade route between Europe and Asia.

Abel Tasman

Tasman is one of Holland's greatest seamen, exploring new trade routes and lands for the Dutch in the Dutch East Indies (now Indonesia). In 1642, he sails south-east from Java to explore the south Pacific. He sights New Zealand and visits Van Diemen's Land (now called Tasmania). Tasman sails around most of mainland Australia without sighting it.

Amerigo Vespucci

This Italian navigator explores the South American coast between 1499 and 1500. In 1508, he becomes the Chief Royal Pilot of Spain. All Spanish sea captains report to him with details of their voyages, which he adds to his maps. Vespucci's maps of the "New World" are so good that sailors call it "Amerigo's Land" or "America."

James Cook

James Cook, an Englishman, is one of the world's greatest maritime explorers and navigators. Between 1768 and 1779, he makes three round-the-world voyages, exploring and charting many areas of the Pacific Ocean. He becomes the first European to visit New Zealand and the eastern coast of Australia. Cook almost travels to Antarctica—he circles the continent, but surrounding ice prevents him from sighting land.

Ferdinand Magellan

Between 1519 and 1522, this Portuguese adventurer proves that the world's oceans are linked by sailing around the world. Unfortunately, he is killed in a battle on the way and never completes the journey himself. Magellan's voyage contributes greatly to knowledge about the earth. It proves the earth is round and not flat. Globes are now used to calculate routes and bearings more accurately.

Sir Francis Drake

Drake is actually an English pirate, who raids Spanish treasure ships. But between 1577 and 1580, he becomes the first Englishman to sail around the world. First of all, Drake sails down the western coast of South America, raiding ships. He fears he will be attacked if he goes back the same way so he decides to sail home by the way of the Pacific and Indian Oceans. It takes him almost three years to sail around the world back to England.

Sea Exploration

Use the text to answer the questions.

1. **Explain what people at the beginning of the millennium knew about other parts of the world.**

   _____
   _____
   _____

2. **Give two reasons why explorers set out on sea voyages.**

   _____
   _____

3. **True or False?**

   (a) Magellan completed his round-the-world journey. ☐ true ☐ false
   (b) Sir Francis Drake was a Spanish pirate. ☐ true ☐ false
   (c) Vasco da Gama sailed around Africa. ☐ true ☐ false
   (d) James Cook discovered Antarctica. ☐ true ☐ false
   (e) Tasman landed on mainland Australia. ☐ true ☐ false
   (f) Dirk Hartog had an island named after him. ☐ true ☐ false

4. **How did America get its name?**

   _____
   _____

5. **Explain how Hartog discovered Australia.**

   _____
   _____
   _____
   _____

6. **Do you think these sailors were brave? Give a reason for your answer.**

   _____
   _____
   _____
   _____
   _____

World Teachers Press® — Exploring Change - Book 2

Sea Exploration

1. Find the nationality of each explorer below and name his country of origin.

Explorer	Nationality	Country
Vespucci		
Tasman		
Cook		
da Gama		

2. An adjective is a word describing a noun. Find the noun in the text these adjectives describe.

   (a) pewter _____
   (b) remarkable _____
   (c) small _____
   (d) treasure _____
   (e) western _____
   (f) next _____

3. Find a word from the text for each suffix.

   –ly _____
   –able _____
   –ish _____
   –er _____
   –ing _____
   –tion _____

4. Write these words in alphabetical order.

   voyage   countries   curiosity   village   civilizations   exploration

   _____
   _____

5. How many compound words can you make with the word "sea"?

6. A proper noun always begins with a capital letter and names a particular person, place, or thing.

   Find proper nouns in the text beginning with these letters.

   S _____
   D _____
   M _____
   A _____
   V _____
   I _____
   N _____
   P _____
   C _____

Sea Exploration

1. Read the extra information about Christopher Columbus and then complete his personal profile.

   Columbus, Christopher (1451 – 1506)

   Columbus was born in the Italian seaport of Genoa. As a youth, he helped his father at the loom of his wool weaving business. However, he had always longed to go to sea, which he eventually did around the age of 20.

   He made many voyages before setting off in 1492 to try to find a shorter route to the Indies—sailing west instead of around Africa. After many months he discovered land, now known as the Bahamas. Columbus made three more voyages of exploration, crossing the Atlantic with the idea of finding a passage to the Indies. He reached the mainland of Central and South America on his third and fourth voyages. He is called the discoverer of America—even though Native Americans had lived there for thousands of years.

   Last name _____

   First name _____

   Age at death _____

   Nationality _____

   Occupation _____

   Greatest Achievement _____

2. (a) Find each explorer in the word search.

   (b) Number each explorer in alphabetical order and write an interesting fact about each one.

I	C	C	U	P	S	E	V	A	A
H	H	D	E	V	A	C	U	P	N
D	M	A	G	E	L	L	A	N	A
R	K	G	R	S	U	B	K	A	M
A	O	A	R	T	V	O	L	A	S
K	O	M	U	P	O	E	L	L	A
E	M	A	O	C	T	G	T	V	T
U	S	U	B	M	U	L	O	C	S

   ☐ Columbus _____

   ☐ da Gama _____

   ☐ Magellan _____

   ☐ Hartog _____

   ☐ Tasman _____

   ☐ Vespucci _____

   ☐ Cook _____

   ☐ Drake _____

Extra: Research another explorer of the sea during the millennium. Complete his/her personal profile using the outline in Question 1.

World Teachers Press®   Exploring Change - Book 2   37

Toys and Games

Toys and games have always played an important role in our lives. They allow us to have fun while learning and developing special skills.

At the beginning of the millennium, you find many of the same toys and games as we have today! Dolls, balls, hoops, hide-and-seek, leapfrog and charades are played by children. They are handmade by craftspeople or parents from wood or other natural materials. Today, toys and games are usually made in factories from synthetic materials such as plastic. Toy manufacturing is a very important industry.

Cards

Cards are first played in China just before the year 1000. They appear in Europe around 1300. Then, they are played by adults—today, children play, too! Among the most popular adult games are bridge, poker and rummy. Still an old favorite of children is snap.

Board games

Chess becomes very popular in Europe from around 1200. The first factory-made board games are holma (1880) and ludo (1898), as well as many others that use dice and counters. The most popular board game to date is Monopoly® (1935). New board games are being invented all the time.

Frisbees®

Throwing a frisbee becomes popular in America in 1947. Students at a university buy pies from the William R. Frisbie bakery. When they finish eating, they throw the tin pie plates to each other. The "Frisbee" is invented! Today, frisbees are made of plastic.

Marbles

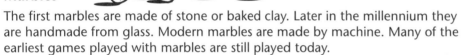

The first marbles are made of stone or baked clay. Later in the millennium they are handmade from glass. Modern marbles are made by machine. Many of the earliest games played with marbles are still played today.

Rollerskates

The first rollerskates are worn by Joseph Merlin in 1760 at a fancy dress ball. He enters the ball on skates, playing a violin at the same time. Merlin is unable to stop and crashes into a mirror! Today, inline skates are more popular.

Hoops

Hoops are a very old toy. Children from all over the world have always played with hoops. Once, they were made of vines, wood or metal. In 1957, a hollow plastic hoop is made. It is named the "Hula Hoop®," after a Hawaiian dance.

The yo-yo

The yo-yo is invented in ancient China, moves to Greece, and is then recorded in India as early as 1765. In 1790, the yo-yo is first seen in Europe. Around the 16th century, Filipinos use yo-yos as weapons to stun prey from trees. The yo-yo has been called the world's most famous toy!

The Barbie® Doll

Barbie is created in 1958 by Elliott and Ruth Handler. She is the first doll to have an adult-shaped body and a complete wardrobe of clothes. Ken®, a male doll, follows later. Barbie and Ken are the names of the inventors' children.

Electronic games

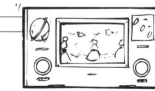

In the 1970s, electronic games are being developed. The first video game is "Pong®," a very simple table tennis game! Since then, there has been rapid growth in electronic and computer games. Some people say too much time and money are spent on electronic games. Others argue they help develop reflexes and concentration, and introduce computers.

Toys and Games

Use the text to answer these questions.

1. **Briefly explain how each toy or game got its name.**

    (a) Barbie® doll _____

    (b) Frisbee® _____

    (c) Hula Hoop® _____

2. **Write fact or opinion.**

    (a) Children will play marbles in the year 2010. _____

    (b) Cards were first played in China. _____

    (c) Computers are too expensive. _____

    (d) Rollerskating is dangerous. _____

    (e) The yo–yo was first invented in ancient China. _____

3. **Write questions for these answers.**

    (a) Stone or baked clay. _____

    (b) Monopoly®. _____

    (c) In the 1970s. _____

    (d) Snap. _____

    (e) Joseph Merlin. _____

4. (a) Draw your favorite toy.   (b) Explain why you like it.

    _____
    _____
    _____
    _____
    _____

Toys and Games

1. Find the opposite of these words from the text.

    (a) new _____ (b) modern _____

    (c) catch _____ (d) few _____

    (e) complex _____ (f) last _____

2. The words below are in the text. Complete the table for each word. Be careful as some are tricky!

		played	
allow			
		invented	
			eating
	crashes		
		spent	
			beginning
appear			
		seen	
argue			

3. Write the number of syllables for each word.

    (a) popular ☐   (b) electronic ☐   (c) mirror ☐

    (d) concentration ☐   (e) plastic ☐   (f) leapfrog ☐

    (g) manufacturing ☐   (h) marbles ☐   (i) chess ☐

    (j) developing ☐   (k) century ☐   (l) created ☐

4. Unjumble these words from the text.

    (a) oyts _____

    (b) uafosm _____

    (c) rpoeumtc _____

    (d) aegsm _____

    (e) ednamhda _____

    (f) odlsl _____

    (g) bdroearw _____

    (h) emrlabs _____

Toys and Games

1. Do you agree or disagree? Complete the debate framework below.

   Topic: *Computers are a waste of time.*

   Arguments for...   Supporting evidence...

   _____   _____
   _____   _____
   _____   _____
   _____   _____
   _____   _____

   Arguments against...   Supporting evidence...

   _____   _____
   _____   _____
   _____   _____
   _____   _____
   _____   _____

   Conclusion

   _____
   _____

2. Write interesting facts in each of the toys below.

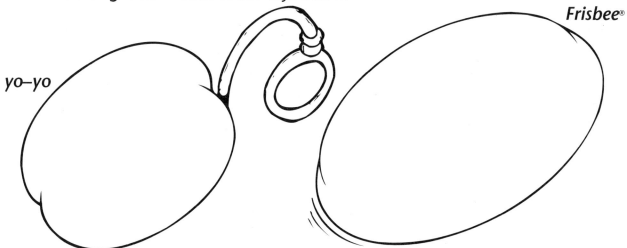

3. (a) On another piece of paper make three lists:

         Board Games   Toys   Games

   (b) Brainstorm as many as you can for each list.

   (c) Circle those you think would have been played in the year 1000.

   (d) Compile a class list of toys.

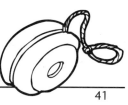

Transportation

At the start of our millennium, people traveled by foot, carrying their possessions, or relied on animals such as horses, oxen, camels, llamas, or elephants for transportation. If they lived near water, they used rafts, canoes, junks, or boats with sails. The fastest form of travel was by sea. Longboats used by the Viking people of Scandinavia traveled about 20 km an hour. Traveling quickly by horseback was about half that speed.

Some significant developments in transportation since 1000 are:

The "Whippletree" (1000s)

A "whippletree" is a pivoted crossbar at the front of a wagon to which harnesses are attached. This allows teams of animals to share the pulling of a wagon instead of just a single animal. Bigger loads can now be transported. Without such a device, a wagon can be thrown off balance or even overturn.

The "Sternpost" Rudder (1000s–1300s)

The Chinese first develop a rudder attached to the stern of a ship before the idea spreads to Europe in the 1300s. This leads to the building of larger ships which cannot be steered properly with oars. During the 1400s shipbuilders build ships four times as large as any built before. They are capable of making long ocean voyages.

Wagons (1400s)

Wagons with a body hung from the main framework are made, giving a more comfortable ride. The wheels often have metal rims, called tires, and studs to prevent them from slipping sideways.

Road Building (1600s–1800s)

Roads are gradually improved for stagecoach services to start. They have solid foundations and curved surfaces, to drain off rain and floodwater. The first public coach services begin in the mid-1700s. The coaches travel in stages and coachmen change the horses. This gives the "stagecoach" its name.

The Submarine (1683)

The first submarines are made of wood. Cornelius Drebbel's is rowed by twelve oarsmen who are supplied air through tubes.

The Steam Engine (1700s–1800s)

This invention brings the biggest change of all in transportation. The age of the train and the steamship has arrived. More people and goods can be transported faster, on land, by rail and on water by steamboats or steamships. However, people still use other sources of power such as animals and the wind.

Hot-air Balloon (1783)

Jacques and Joseph Montgolfier send up the first hot-air balloon with people on board. It drifts across Paris for about 25 minutes before landing safely.

The Motor Car (1885)

In 1880, there were no cars in the world. Now there are more than 100 million! The world's first gasoline-powered car is built by Karl Benz in 1885.

The First Airplane Flight (1903)

The first airplane to lift a person into the air and fly successfully is made by the Wright brothers. It flies 37 meters at Kitty Hawk, North Carolina. The plane stays airborne for 12 seconds. By the end of the day, it flies for a full minute!

Apollo 11 Moon Landing (1969)

A rocket is developed that can fly humans to the moon and back. Neil Armstrong is the first man to set foot on the moon in July 1969. The three astronauts onboard *Apollo 11* bring back pieces of the moon for scientific study.

At the end of our millennium, we have many forms of transportation—bullet trains, space shuttles, hydrofoils and hovercraft, to name just a few.

Transportation

Use the text to answer these questions.

1. **Explain how people traveled by land and water around the year 1000.**

   (a) by land… _____
   _____
   _____
   _____

   (b) by water… _____
   _____
   _____
   _____

2. **Why is the steam engine such an important invention?**
   _____
   _____
   _____
   _____

3. **List some developments in transportation under the following headings.**

Land	Sea	Air

4. **True or False?**

   (a) Roads were well made in 1200. _____

   (b) The first submarines were made of steel. _____

   (c) Large ships can be steered properly with a rudder. _____

   (d) Wagons were more comfortable after 1400. _____

   (e) Most developments in air transportation came before 1800. _____

Transportation

1. Find the dictionary meaning for these words from the text.

    (a) possessions _____

    (b) pivot _____

    (c) junk _____

    (d) stern _____

2. Write three compound words from the text.

3. Complete the syllable chart below with words from the text.

Two syllables	Three syllables	Four or more syllables

4. Find antonyms for these from the text.

    (a) finish _____

    (b) few _____

    (c) smallest _____

    (d) double _____

    (e) last _____

    (f) after _____

5. Use a dictionary to help you find word builders for these by adding prefixes and suffixes.

    (a) carry _____

    (b) develop _____

    (c) transport _____

6. How many words can you make from the letters in "transportation"?

    Use the back of this sheet to list them.

Transportation

1. **Design a form of transportation for the new millennium. You will need to consider the following:**
   - will it be used on land, sea, air, or a combination of these?
   - how it will be powered?
   - size, color, shape
   - who will use it?

   Draw your design, label each part and explain how it is used.

   _____
   _____

2. **Choose one of the developments in transportation. Imagine you are a reporter witnessing the event for the first time. Plan your story under the headings below.**

who ...	what ...	when ...
where ...	why ...	conclusion ...

   Headline

   $1.50   ♦ THE NEWS TODAY ♦   Date:_____

Answers

Authors 6 – 9

page 7
1. Teacher check
2. Rudyard Kipling, 1907
3. (a) Australian bush
   (b) English country life
   (c) Australian outback
   (d) 19th century life
4. Teacher check
5. Sir Thomas More—falls from favor and is executed for treason.
6. *English Poets* – Geoffrey Chaucer, William Shakespeare
   Children's Authors – Mark Twain, AA Milne, Hans Christian Andersen, Lewis Carroll, Rudyard Kipling
   Australian Authors – Banjo Paterson, Henry Lawson
7. (a) Lewis Carroll (b) George Orwell
   (c) Mark Twain   (d) Banjo Paterson

page 8
1. (a) the qualities of courtesy and bravery
   (b) a humorous way of speaking in which the real meaning is the opposite of what is said
   (c) a state of sleepy laziness
   (d) description in words
   (e) modest and meek
2. (a) early   (b) short
   (c) best   (d) known
   (e) rich   (f) unforgettable
3. (a) varied   (b) brilliant
   (c) prolific   (d) witty
   (e) tales   (f) essays
4. *Animal Farm, Just So Stories, Oliver Twist, Romeo and Juliet, Wind in the Willows, Winnie the Pooh*
5. Teacher check
6. (a) 3 (b) 3 (c) 2 (d) 4 (e) 2
   (f) 1 (g) 2 (h) 3 (i) 4

page 9
1. Teacher check
2. Teacher check
3. Teacher check
4. Teacher check

Clothing 10 – 13

page 11
1. protection, modesty, fashion
2. changing lifestyles and fashions
3. (a) false   (b) true   (c) true
   (d) true   (e) false (f) false
4. Teacher check
5. Many new skills and ideas were introduced with increasing trade with other countries.
6. Women's dresses are shorter and men's suits are less "fussy."
7. Teacher check

page 12
1. (a) showing proper and decent behavior
   (b) any woven material used for clothing, curtains, etc.
   (c) made in large quantities with machines in factories
   (d) made by human beings
   (e) fine threads of wool, cotton, or other material
2. Teacher check
3. Teacher check
4. (a) simpler   (b) protection
   (c) trousers   (d) flourish
   (e) care   (f) decorative
5. (a) children's clothes
   (b) a lady's hat
   (c) the boy's shirt
   (d) a lord's tunic
   (e) the girl's dress
   (f) ladies' bags
   (g) women's shoes
   (h) a worker's uniform
   (i) men's trousers
   (j) a child's coat

page 13
1. (a) 1000 – 1500, Teacher check
   (b) 1500 – 1850, Teacher check
   (c) 1850 – today, Teacher check
2. Teacher check

Communication 14 – 17

page 15
1. Information was spread by word of mouth or written out by hand.
2. (a) goose feathers
   (b) developing the steam engine
3. Johannes **Gutenberg**, who invented the first **printing press** in 1454, was a **German** metalsmith. He casts individual raised **metal** letters and **coats** them with an **oily** ink. The **letters** are then stamped onto **paper** with a screw press. Although **books** can now be produced more **quickly** and **easily** they are still very **expensive**.
4. Christopher Sholes redesigned the keyboard layout so it became easier to type quickly.
5. (a) word processor   (b) photocopier
6. He invented a method of writing rapidly by using symbols or letters to represent the sounds of words.

page 16
1. (a) which   (b) too   (c) not
   (d) lead   (e) steel (f) through
2. Teacher check
3. (a) the crime of making an imitation and passing it off as genuine
   (b) cut with a sharp tool
   (c) movements of part of your body to express feelings
   (d) a soft blackish form of carbon used in lead pencils
4. (a) drawn   (b) cards
   (c) ink, think   (d) making
   (e) mouth   (f) steam
5. (a) placed, place, lace, aced, ace
   (b) draw, wings, raw, wing, win, in
   (c) type, writers, writer, write, writ, it
6. revolutionizes

page 17
1. 1 – Printed books…
   2 – Playing cards appear…
   3 – The first printing press…
   4 – The first pencils…
   5 – The first office copier…
   6 – The steam-powered press…
   7 – The system of shorthand…
   8 – Typewriters are first…
   9 – Ladislo Biro's ballpoint…
   10 – Electrostatic photocopying…
   11 – First word processors…
   12 – Desktop computers…
2. Teacher check
3. (a) false   (b) true
   (c) false   (d) false
   (e) Chester F. Carlson
   (f) ballpoint pen, electrostatic photocopying, word processor, desktop computer, laser printer
   (g) Johannes Gutenberg, Fredrick König

Cooking 18 – 21

page 19
1. (a) 1937   (b) 1910
   (c) 1909   (d) 1980s
2. (a) Denis Papin
   (b) Robert Bunsen
   (c) Dr. Percy Spencer
3. (a) opinion   (b) opinion
   (c) fact   (d) fact
4. in kettles or on spits in their fireplace
5. by using radio waves that penetrate the food and vibrate its molecules, producing heat by friction, which cooks the food
6. Teacher check
7. Teacher check

page 20
1. convection, cooker, electric, fireplace, gas, microwave, oven
2. (a) the smallest unit or particle into which something can be divided
   (b) to keep on moving quickly up and down or to and fro
   (c) the rubbing of one thing against another
   (d) to go into or through
   (e) having to do with actual practice or action, rather than ideas
   (f) to move in a circle or circuit
3. Teacher check
4. (a) pen, net, rate, rat, ate, at
   (b) fire, ire, places, place, laces, lace, aces, ace
   (c) invent, in, vent, on
   (d) under, standing, stand, and, din, in, an
5. (a) team, tame, mate   (b) mite, emit
   (c) saw   (d) sag

page 21
1. Teacher check
2. Teacher check
3. Teacher check

Energy 22 – 25

page 23
1. Possible answers – sun, human, muscles, fire, animal, power, animal dung, charcoal, coal, animal oils, water power and wind power
2. Thomas Savery – to draw water up from mines.
3. This is heat from the Earth itself—such as steam expelled from volcanic holes.
4. Teacher check

Answers

5. (a) electricity generated from falling or running water
   (b) forcing atoms to release energy by exposing them to extreme heat
   (c) heat from the earth used as a power source
   (d) once called dynamos, they generate the power for most electrical sources
   (e) convert sunlight directly into electricity
6. Teacher check

page 24
1. Teacher check
2. gas, generate, geothermal, given, go, great
3. (a) noisy (b) always (c) release
   (d) efficient (e) first (f) before
4. Teacher check
5. Teacher check
6. reactor, discover/ed, becomes release, distribute, begins

page 25
1. Teacher check
2. 1698 – steam-powered
   1709 – charcoal
   1859 – Edwin Drake drills first oil well in America.
   1873 – Electricity, dynamos
   1881 – hydroelectric
   1904 – geothermal energy
   1945 – Petroleum gas
   1955 – Solar cells, sun
   1975 – Alcohol, sugar cane, motor vehicles
   1982 – Wind power, Washington
   1990s – Fusion
3. Teacher check

Farming 26 – 29

page 27
1. Teacher check
2. turnips
3. It reaps, threshes, stores the grain and makes hay bales while crossing a field.
4. buckets, hand-operated pumps, huge sprinkler systems
5. (a) true (b) false
   (c) true (d) true
   (e) false (f) true
6. Teacher check

page 28
1. (a) Meat from slaughtered animals is dried or salted.
   (b) The seed drill allows grain to be planted in rows.
2. (a) tomatoes (b) grains
   (c) turnips (d) potatoes
   (e) knives (f) chemicals
   (g) children (h) sheep
3. (a) tiny sprinkler system
   (b) carts easier to move
   (c) quickly becomes a staple food
   (d) positive effects on the environment
4. (a) older (b) meat
   (c) breed (d) bales
   (e) plows (f) trend
5. Teacher check
6. Teacher check

page 29
1. Teacher check
2.

H	I	R	R	I	G	A	T	I	O	N	P
S	H	F	E	R	T	I	L	I	Z	E	R
L	A	A	A	G	R	A	I	N	D	Y	O
A	R	R	P	L	A	P	L	O	W	G	H
M	V	M	E	B	C	M	D	E	E	S	A
I	E	E	R	E	T	S	T	O	C	K	Y
N	S	R	R	E	O	P	I	N	R	U	T
A	T	S	G	F	R	L	L	I	R	D	N

Medicine 30 - 33

page 31
1. (a) makes surgery safer by using carbolic acid to clean instruments and dressings
   (b) shows how the heart and blood vessels work to circulate blood through the body
   (c) develops the process called vaccination
   (d) discovers x-rays
2. Parts inside the human body too small to be seen can now be operated on.
3. Medicine practiced with magic, witchcraft and astrology.
4. Teacher check
5. By taking more vitamin C such as in lime juice
6. ether, William Morten, 1846
   human anatomy, Andreas Vesalius, 1500s
   first heart transplant, Dr. Christaan Barnard, 1967
   blood circulation, William Harvey, 1628
   inoculation, Edward Jenner, 1796
   heart-lung machine, Dr. John Gibbon, 1953
7. Teacher check

page 32
1. (a) a drug capable of killing bacteria and other germs
   (b) a strong germ-fighting substance
   (c) microscopic living bodies that can cause disease and decay
   (d) sound vibrations used to treat or investigate internal parts of the body
2. (a) instrument, in, strum, rum, men, me
   (b) perform, formed, form, for, or, me
   (c) some, thing, so, thin, in, met, me
   (d) small, pox, mall, all, ox
3.

great	greater	greatest
early	earlier	earliest
small	smaller	smallest
rare	rarer	rarest
mean	meaner	meanest
mild	milder	mildest

4. brain, disease, doctor, genetic, resistance, safer, scanning, scurvy, vaccination
5. (a) 4 (b) 3 (c) 1
   (d) 2 (e) 3 (f) 4
   (g) 4 (h) 2 (i) 1
   (j) 4 (k) 2 (l) 4
6. (a) Blood vessels circulate blood though the body.
   (b) Carbolic acid is used to clean instruments and dressings.

page 33
1. Teacher check
2. Teacher check

Sea Exploration 34 – 37

page 35
1. They knew very little about what existed more that a few days' journey from where they live.
2. curiosity, search for trade
3. (a) false (b) false (c) true
   (d) false (e) false (f) true
4. Sailors called it "Amerigo's Land" or "America" after Amerigo Vespucci who made excellent maps of the coast.
5. Hartog was sailing to the Dutch East Indies when he sailed too far east and sighted land off the western coast of Australia.
6. Teacher check

page 36
1. Italian, Italy
   Dutch, Holland
   British, England
   Portuguese, Portugal
2. (a) plate (b) voyages
   (c) place, fleet (d) ships
   (e) coast (f) town
3. Teacher check
4. civilizations, countries, curiosity, exploration, village, voyage
5. Teacher check
6. Teacher check

page 37
1. Teacher check
2. (a)

2. (b) Columbus, Cook, da Gama, Drake, Hartog, Magellan, Tasman, Vespucci

Toys and Games 38 – 41

page 39
1. (a) Named after the inventors' two children.
   (b) Named after William R. Frisbie who owned the bakery where pie tins were purchased.
   (c) Named after a Hawaiian dance.
2. (a) opinion (b) fact (c) opinion
   (d) opinion (e) fact
3. Teacher check
4. (a) Teacher check
   (b) Teacher check

Answers

page 40
1. (a) old (b) ancient (c) throw
   (d) many (e) simple (f) first
2. Teacher check
3. (a) 3 (b) 4 (c) 2 (d) 4
   (e) 2 (f) 2 (g) 5 (h) 2
   (i) 1 (j) 4 (k) 3 (l) 3
4. (a) toys (b) famous
   (c) computer (d) games
   (e) handmade (f) dolls
   (g) wardrobe (h) marbles

page 41
1. Teacher check
2. Teacher check
3. Teacher check

Transportation 42 – 45

page 43
1. (a) People traveled by foot, carrying their possessions or used animals such as horses, oxen, camels, llamas, or elephants.
   (b) People used rafts, canoes, junks, or boats with sails.
2. Steam-powered engines allowed more people and goods to be transported faster on land, by rail, or on water.
3. Teacher check
4. (a) false (b) false (c) true
   (d) true (e) false

page 44
1. (a) your property or wealth; the things you own
   (b) something on which something turns
   (c) a Chinese flat-bottomed boat
   (d) the back part of a boat
2. Teacher check
3. Teacher check
4. (a) start (b) many
   (c) biggest (d) single
   (e) first (f) before
5. Teacher check
6. Teacher check

page 45
1. Teacher check
2. Teacher check